Images of America
Calvin Coolidge's Plymouth, Vermont

IMAGES of America
CALVIN COOLIDGE'S PLYMOUTH, VERMONT

J.R. Greene

First published 1997
Copyright © J.R. Greene, 1997

ISBN 0-7524-0945-7

Published by Arcadia Publishing,
an imprint of the Chalford Publishing Corporation,
One Washington Center, Dover, New Hampshire 03820.
Printed in Great Britain

Library of Congress Cataloging-in-Publication Data applied for

A Note on Coolidge Family Names

President Coolidge's family was much enamored of the names John and Calvin, perhaps in honor of the pioneer Protestant theologian. One or another, or both of these names appear in several generations of the family. To avoid confusion, each family member is identified in the text by a specific name.

The president was born with the name John Calvin Coolidge, after his father. However, he dropped his first name by the time he became a lawyer, so he is referred to as Calvin Coolidge, or the president. The president's grandfather was Calvin Galusha Coolidge. The president's father was John C. Coolidge. The president's two sons were John Coolidge and Calvin Coolidge Jr.

Contents

Preface   7

Brief History of Plymouth   9

1. Plymouth Outside of the Notch   11

2. Plymouth Notch   35

3. Calvin Coolidge in Plymouth   73

Sources   128

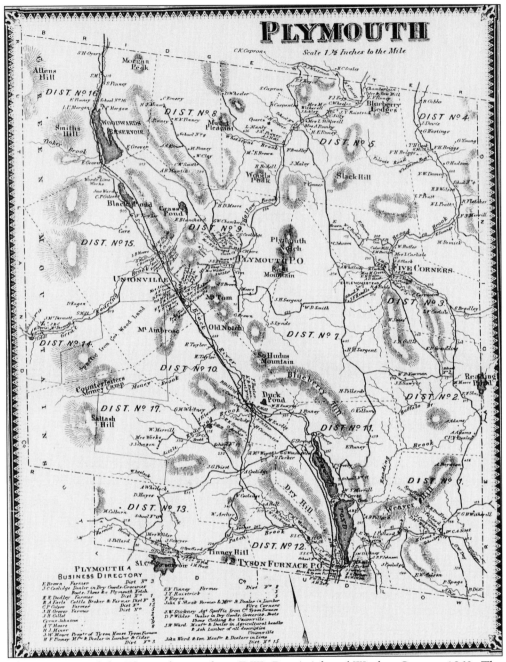

This is a copy of the Plymouth map from *F.W. Beers' Atlas of Windsor County*, 1869. The numerous hachure-marks emphasize the hilly character of the town. The railroad shown on the map was never built.

Preface

This book is meant to convey a pictorial record of the town of Plymouth, Vermont. A small town, nestled in the hills in the central part of the state, Plymouth is typical of many rural New England communities, yet it has special features of interest.

The most well-known fact about Plymouth is that it was the birthplace and childhood home of Calvin Coolidge, the 30th president of the United States. While the visitors' center and well-preserved sites relating to Coolidge's life are the major factors drawing visitors to Plymouth, the town is an attractive community in many other ways.

Plymouth still has cleared open spaces, reminiscent of its agricultural past, as well as many well-preserved old homes and farmsteads to please the eye of the beholder. A state forest provides campsites and hiking trails for those who enjoy the outdoors, and major ski areas are located in adjoining towns. Plymouth has many summer camps, beaches on some of its ponds, and fine lodgings for travelers.

A study of the history of Plymouth reveals a chronicle of events similar to many other Vermont towns: the coming and going of numerous small industries, the quarrying of marble, isolation due to being bypassed by railroads, the loss of population after the Civil War to better opportunities in the west, and the slow revival of the town via the tourist trade in the early 1900s (even before Calvin Coolidge became a national figure).

However, Plymouth also saw some phenomena unusual in rural New England. A literal gold rush took place on streams in parts of the town around the Civil War. The Tyson iron furnace produced a number of products in the middle 1800s. A large limestone cavern is located in the northern part of town. A "counterfeiters money camp" is supposed to have existed in the early 1800s in the west part of Plymouth. Besides Calvin Coolidge, the town has produced an attorney general (John G. Sargent), a Vermont governor (William Stickney), a noted dwarf (Dan McCuin), and a famed nineteenth-century lecturer and healer (Achsa Sprague).

The focus of this book is the era of Calvin Coolidge, from the 1880s until the 1930s. All of the illustrations in this book are from the author's collection; most are reproduced from old postcards. While an attempt has been made to avoid using illustrations that have appeared in previous works about Plymouth or Coolidge, this has been unavoidable in a few instances. Many of these views were taken by Vermont photographers L.F. Brehmer, George Chalmers, or Henry W. Richardson. While other sections of the town of Plymouth are included here, the emphasis is upon Coolidge's native village of Plymouth Notch.

The author wishes to thank the following for providing facts used in compiling some of the captions in this book: William W. Jenney (regional historic site administrator at Plymouth Notch) and Eliza Ward (a Plymouth historian). The author would like to acknowledge the assistance of Jay Clark (Ludlow, VT) in obtaining some of the illustrations used in this book. Thanks are also due to Les Campbell of Sky Meadow Gallery (Belchertown, MA) for developing photographs out of old negatives for use in this book.

It is the sincere hope of the author that the reader will enjoy this trip back in time to a different era and another place, which combined to foster the growth of a man who became president of the United States during one of the country's more prosperous periods.

J.R. Greene
June 1997

A Brief History of Plymouth

Plymouth, VT, was known as Saltash when it received a charter from the Colony of New Hampshire on July 6, 1761. The first settler in the town was John Mudge, from Fitchburg, Massachusetts. The town was formally organized in 1787, when it contained about fifteen families. Among the first town officials were John Coolidge (ancestor of the president), a captain in the Revolutionary War, who had moved here from Lancaster, Massachusetts.

The town's name was changed to Plymouth in 1797. In the census of 1800, its population had risen to 497. Population would peak at 1,417 in 1840. Numbers fell to a low of 283 in 1970, but rebounded to 440 in 1990.

Plymouth, in the western part of Windsor County, is 22,249 acres in extent, and is roughly square in shape. It is bordered by Sherburne and Bridgewater on the north, Reading and Cavendish on the east, Ludlow and Mt. Holly on the south, and Shrewsbury and Mendon on the west.

Plymouth was primarily an agricultural community during its first 150 years. Many small industries flourished here during the middle 1800s, most involving wood products or local minerals. Limestone, marble, iron, and even some gold were extracted from the soil, especially in the southern and eastern parts of town. The village of Tyson grew up around an iron furnace established by Isaac Tyson in the 1830s.

Around the time of the Civil War, Plymouth had seventeen district schools and an academy at the Union village. Several villages were scattered around the town: Tyson, Plymouth Union, Plymouth Notch, Frog City, The Kingdom, Five Corners, and Pinney Hollow. Besides a school, many of these had a sawmill or gristmill.

The decline of many of the local industries, added to the attraction of better agricultural lands in the west, caused Plymouth to steadily lose population after the Civil War. Outside of the occasional employment that the small mills or lumbering provided, farming was the last remaining occupation for most inhabitants of the town. E.E. Whiting, a Boston newsman who visited the town in 1920, referred to it as "an inspiring country in the majesty of its hills, and in the tremendous silence . . . a positive, assertive silence."

A boom in tourism hit the town with the ascension of Calvin Coolidge to the presidency on August 3, 1923. Besides storekeeper Florence Cilley, others in the village catered to tourists by selling food, souvenirs, and gifts. The Civilian Conservation Corps did reforestation work in the 1930s, which assisted the establishment of the Coolidge State Forest and its campground. Tourism is still a major industry in the town, with several inns joining the campground in offering accommodations. Plymouth's several lakes, the proximity of major ski areas (including a small one in Plymouth) and antique businesses, and cultural activities in nearby Woodstock have all bolstered Plymouth's attraction for tourists. Many summer homes and camps are located within the town.

In spite of all this activity, Plymouth still retains some of its late-nineteenth-century rural character, especially at the Notch village. Even the visitors' center there was built with the old-fashioned "sneckered ashlar" stone exterior to fit in with the original buildings nearby. Almost all of the buildings from Calvin Coolidge's time are still standing and several are open to the public. Plymouth Notch is now a living museum. Most of the rest of the town remains the quiet place it always has been; a place that is relatively "silent."

One
Plymouth Outside of the Notch

Located near the old Crown Point military road, the remains of this lime kiln were photographed in the 1920s. Col. John C. Coolidge, the president's father, reportedly earned his first $100 "burning out" lime in a similar kiln. This one was located in the former village of Plymouth Kingdom, in the southeast corner of town. The Kingdom was the first part of town to be settled in the late 1700s. At one time, it had several small mills, a store, school, and a church. There are now only a few private homes in this neighborhood.

This stone monument was erected near Amherst Lake in 1926, by the Lucy Fletcher Chapter of the Daughters of the American Revolution. It marks a spot on the route of the Crown Point military road, the first road in Plymouth. It was built through the southern part of town over an old Native American trail, under the direction of General Jeffrey Amherst in 1759–60, at the time of his expedition to capture Crown Point, on Lake Champlain, during the French and Indian War. The bronze plaque on the marker notes that the 26-mile encampment was a 1/4 mile west of it.

Amherst Lake (or Lake Amherst) is the northernmost lake of the two on the Black River at the southern end of town. Known as Upper Plymouth Pond before 1886, it was renamed for General Amherst, who laid out the military road on the east and north sides of this lake. Many summer camps may now be found on its shores.

This old red mill once stood just below the outlet of Amherst Lake. Corn, wheat, and oats were ground here on three water wheels. The mill had a reputation for never running dry, as it had the whole lake to draw water from.

Echo Lake is the lower of the two lakes on the Black River just above Tyson village. This lake provided waterpower for the mills in that village. It was known as Lower Plymouth or Tyson Pond before the late 1800s. Today, many summer camps line its shore.

Ice races were occasionally held on Echo Lake. Horse-drawn sleighs raced along plowed-out "tracks."

Photographers were charmed by scenery on the "Presidential Drive" (Route 100) along the west shore of Echo Lake, and many produced postcards of the views. The noted colorized printmaker David Davidson issued scenes similar to this one.

These houses were located on the east side of Echo Lake, on the road to the Kingdom village. The two houses on the left were owned by Ethel Hill and Mary Dillon, who had successful careers in politics and business, respectively. The one in the right foreground was the James W. Stickney place, which then belonged to the Moriartys.

Vermont Governor (1900–1902) William Stickney lived in this home on the west shore of Echo Lake. It had been built by his father in the 1870s. Stickney had a law practice in nearby Ludlow.

This business, on the shore of Echo Lake, took advantage of the traffic passing by on the way to the president's home village.

The village of Tyson, just south of Echo Lake, grew up in the mid-1800s around Isaac Tyson's iron mill. Alonzo Hubbard was a manufacturer and lumberman in Tyson in the late 1800s. This building housed his combination store and post office, which is no longer standing. The upper part of the Echo Lake Inn is on the left.

The Tyson House, one of two hotels in this village, once stood on this site. In 1888, Alonzo Hubbard tore it down, and erected the more commodious Echo Lake Hotel on the site. It has served as a resort hotel since then, even hosting Henry Ford and Thomas Edison when they visited President Coolidge in 1924.

This c. 1910 view shows a group enjoying a summer day on the piazza at the Echo Lake Hotel. Many of the men sitting in front are dressed in baseball uniforms.

Camp Plymouth, on the eastern shore of Echo Lake, is now a state park. In August 1938, the sender of this view postcard reported "having an awful time here because it is so dull."

In this view at Camp Plymouth, the Boy Scouts are at a flag-raising (or lowering) ceremony. Notice the teepee in the right background.

Plymouth Union reportedly got its name from a union store. This c. 1915 view of the village is looking west, down the notch road. The old blacksmith shop is visible at the right. Moore's Hall and Store (now the Salt Ash Inn) are behind the shop. The Wilder House Hotel is the building in the left background.

This view of Plymouth Union is looking down the hill from the western side of the village, down the Shrewsbury Mountain road. Part of the Wilder house is visible at the right.

Levi Moore was the Union village's version of John C. Coolidge. His store carried all kinds of merchandise, and he served as a constable and tax collector. This building was originally two stories high; the peaked roof was raised up before 1900. A hall here was used for local activities, and part of the building served as a hotel, which is now called the Salt Ash Inn.

Moore's store is shown here in an earlier view, taken from further away. The directional sign at the center marks the roads to Ludlow (right) and to Sherburne (left). The open shed on the left is no longer standing.

The small Union village "common" is visible in this 1906 view, which is looking north. Part of the Wilder house can be seen at the left, while the old open shed of Moore's buildings is on the right. Moore and Hayward, Rutland photographers, published this postcard scene.

The Wilder House Hotel, built in the middle 1800s, also contained D.P. Wilder's Hall. Many meetings, dances, and suppers were held here over the years. The back portion of this building was torn down around World War II, and the porch is also gone. The remaining section is now a home.

This 1920s view looks up the road from the Union to the Notch. Moore's store is on the left, with a sign for Coon's Ice Cream. E.B. Horton's store (on the right) sports a Texaco fuel sign, as well as ads for spark plugs and tobacco products on the side wall. This building is now a residence.

The Union village housed a district school, and for many years after the Civil War the Vermont Liberal Institute. This academy was located just south of the Wilder house. M.K. Headle was the principal in the early 1880s. John G. Sargent, who served under President Coolidge as U.S. attorney general, attended this school. Calvin Coolidge acted in a play performed here during the winter of 1891. This view was taken c. 1915. A small home now stands on this site.

The horse-drawn stage is shown here at Plymouth Union. This brought passengers from Ludlow (10 miles away), through here to Woodstock (12 miles away), and back. A one-way trip lasted five hours. Many summer visitors came to Plymouth from the railroad depots in those two towns on this conveyance.

This primitive bridge crossed the Black River at Plymouth Union. A mill dam upstream from here provided waterpower for nearby grist and woodworking mills. This view of two women crossing the bridge in a buggy was taken in 1909.

In this 1920s view, Art Mayo is using his team of horses to draw ice from Moore's Pond, a small body of water near Plymouth Union. He would then deliver it to the Cilley store at Plymouth Notch, where it was stored in the basement to keep things cold in the warmer months.

This 1920s view of North Street in the Union is just north of the crossroads. The home on the left was owned in turn by Damon, Ward, and Skinner. The one in the center was once the home of John Pierce, an undertaker.

Black Pond is located north of Plymouth Union, near Route 100. The gingerbread-style house overlooking the pond was built by Charles and Sarah Gilson. It replaced an earlier homestead which was razed when the pond level was elevated early in the 1900s.

The "last log cabin in Plymouth" was located in the Lynds Hill section of town, which was between Plymouth Notch and the Five Corners villages. John Lynds, a Civil War veteran, lived here. Although quite intact at the time this photograph was taken in the 1920s, it is now gone.

Five Corners village was in the eastern part of Plymouth. In the middle 1800s, it housed sawmills and gristmills, a factory making chairs and tubs, a blacksmith shop, and District School #3. Gold mining was carried on here before and after the Civil War. Most of the buildings seen in this old stereoscopic view are no longer standing.

Timber harvesting has been a major activity in Plymouth, as much of the town's landscape is covered with trees. Wintertime was the best season for this, as the logs could be hauled off the site by ox-drawn sleighs. This scene, taken during the 1920s, shows one of the many sawmills that operated in Plymouth over the years. In 1883, there were ten of them operating in the town—the most of any town in Windsor County. Some of the wood was used in local factories. The open shed shown here housed the saws.

Heavy rains caused severe flooding in many parts of Vermont in 1927. Since Plymouth was a sparsely settled upland community, it did not suffer as much damage as other places, but road washouts like the one pictured here occurred in several places in town.

Calvin Coolidge viewed the damage from the 1927 flood late that summer in Cavendish, a few miles downstream from Plymouth on the Black River.

The Captain John Coolidge House was located in the southwest part of town known as Frog City. It was already falling into ruin when this photograph was taken in the 1920s. One of the first frame houses in town, it was built by Captain Coolidge for his son Luther, shortly after 1820. Later it was known as the McWain place.

This view shows some of the elaborate stenciling on the walls of the interior of the Captain John Coolidge House. All that remains of the house now is its cellarhole.

Pinney Hollow is located in the northeast part of Plymouth, on what is now Route 100A. It was named for Johnathan Pinney, an early settler. A sawmill and a quarry were located here. Calvin Coolidge's mother was born in this neighborhood. Clarence Blanchard owned the home when this view was taken c. 1925.

Pinney Hollow's District #5 School, its teacher, and her scholars are shown here during the spring term of 1898. John C. Coolidge, the president's father, once taught school here in the 1860s.

Dan McCuin lived with his brother in a house in the Frog City section of town, on Route 100. As he was only 31 inches tall as an adult, he was pronounced "the Smallest Man in New England." He posed for several pictures with President Coolidge, of which he sold copies to tourists.

Plymouth Reservoir has also been called Woodward Reservoir or Timberlake. It is located along Route 100 in the northwest corner of town, and is a feeder of the Ottaquechee River. Two institutional summer camps are located near it.

Located in the northwest part of town, Sherburne Hollow is just downstream from the Plymouth Reservoir. In the middle 1800s, it boasted a few farms, a sawmill, and a district school. By the time this picture was taken in the 1920s, only a few of the dwellings were left.

The Civilian Conservation Corps was a New Deal program to put unemployed young men to work in reforestation projects. A camp with several barracks was located in Plymouth, and the tents for this camp are shown here. Some of the work was done in the Calvin Coolidge State Forest, including the establishment of the current campground.

Most of the CCC men in this picture seem glad to have a job, or they may be simply enjoying the outdoor life.

This view was taken inside of the cook tent for the CCC camp. Whether the bearded gentleman is an assistant, or merely an onlooker, is not known.

Two
Plymouth Notch

A notch is a common New England term for a small pass between two hills or mountains. In Plymouth, the term refers both to the pass (now Route 100A) and the village itself, which is nestled among several hills. This view is looking up the notch roadway, which was (and is) narrow, steep, and curvy.

This 1920s view shows an instance when the mail truck failed to navigate a curve on the road between the Union and the Notch.

The Notch cemetery was located on a knoll about a 1/4 mile south of the village. Several generations of Calvin Coolidge's family are buried here, as can be seen to the right in this early 1920s view.

Plymouth Notch's appearance hasn't changed much over the years, as this charming winter scene from c. 1880 proves. From left to right are the Wilder house and barn, Coolidge homestead, a barn on the site of the current cheese factory, the store building, the church, a blacksmith shop, and the stone village school.

This view of Plymouth is from the southwest. The second village schoolhouse is partially visible at the far left. The long house just to the right of the school was the home of Achsa Sprague (1828–1862), a lecturer, preacher, healer, and poet; it is no longer standing. On the right are the church, store building, and the Aldrich home.

This c. 1900 view is looking down Schoolhouse Hill. The second village schoolhouse is the building on the right. Just to the left of that is the cheese factory. Part of the west end of the Coolidge homestead is visible to the left of the factory.

Although taken in the 1920s, this view is recognizable today. This is the road off Route 100A, which goes up a slight incline to the Notch village. From the left are the church, store-post office, Wilder house, and Wilder barn. Calvin Coolidge's mother grew up in the Wilder house. The small Aldrich home can be seen in front of the barn.

This *c.* 1906 view is looking south from in front of the Wilder barn. The elm, and the store-post office, are visible. The carriage shed is attached to the store building on the left side. The ridge south of the village is in the background.

In the late 1800s, Calvin Coolidge's stepmother, Carrie Brown Coolidge, lived here. From 1924 to 1942, Ruth Aldrich used part of this home for a gift shop and small restaurant, calling it "Top of the Notch." She is the woman on the left in this view. Aldrich later had several tourist cabins built behind this. Her home is now the Plymouth Historic Site office.

The road up Schoolhouse Hill is the focus of this charming winter view. From the left are the store-post office, the church, the cheese factory, the Coolidge homestead, and the Wilder house (partly visible on the far right).

The Pinney Hollow Reunion, which met every August between 1897 and 1917, was made up of former residents of that village in the northeast part of Plymouth. In this c. 1900 view, they are posed in front of the elm and store at the Notch.

Old Home Day is a rural New England tradition, usually held during the summer. A small fair is held, with former residents invited back to visit. The Plymouth Old Home Association ran these for a number of years. This one, held on August 16, 1902, featured a basket lunch. The crowd is gathered on the small green between the store and the Wilder house.

This is the program for the event pictured above. Florence Cilley, secretary for the association, was later the storekeeper for many years.

Old Home Week
in Vermont,
August 10 to 16, 1902.

The Plymouth Old Home Association most cordially invite you to return and participate in the observance of Old Home Week, and especially to be present at Plymouth's "Old Home Day," August 16.

Alonzo F. Hubbard, President.
Florence V. Cilley, Secretary.

Basket Lunch.

Scenes such as these became common at Plymouth Notch during the presidency of Calvin Coolidge. The crowd in front of the Wilder house and barn is probably waiting for an opportunity to glance at or shake hands with the president.

In this c. 1927 view, an early tour bus stopped in front of the Wilder barn. No doubt the group went to the store for refreshments, then walked over to look at the Coolidge homestead, and the president's birthplace, in back of the store.

The morning Calvin Coolidge became president, the telephone company strung a line directly to the Coolidge homestead for his use. The pole in front of the Wilder barn is shown here. John C. Coolidge saw no need to keep the phone after his son left that day for Washington, D.C., so he had the line removed!

This building housed the store and post office for most of the time between the mid-1800s and the mid-1900s. John C. Coolidge owned this for nearly fifty years, and ran the store for a decade. He added the second story in 1886. Later owners were Florence Cilley, and Herman and Violet Pelkey. The State of Vermont owns the building, which houses a recreated country store, and a post office. This c. 1913 view shows some women in front of the store.

In most rural New England villages, the general store was a gathering place for swapping news, especially during the winter. This group is keeping warm around the wood stove. Seated from the left are Herb Moore, Florence Cilley, and her ward, Violet Hickory Pelkey. The man seated second from the right is John Wilder.

The variety of goods carried in this "country store" is suggested by this scene. Besides the dry goods on the shelves, various souvenirs, including felt pennants, can be seen. The counter at the bottom contains stacks of postcards, which sold at prices ranging from 2¢ to 5¢ each.

Even though a truck replaced the old horse-drawn vehicle delivering mail to the store after World War I, the vehicle was still called the "stage." In earlier years, the arrival of the mail was a highlight of the day in the village.

One winter, an experiment to use skis on the front of a car was tried for the stage. When that vehicle kept sliding into ditches, it was altered by using tractor wheels on the back end, as shown here.

Ordinary automobiles sometimes visited the store in winter. The man in this view is unknown; Florence Cilley is next to him. To her right is her ward, Violet Hickory Pelkey.

Like most small stores, Plymouth's had a number of items delivered directly by jobbers or wholesalers. This one supplied Verso Cigars.

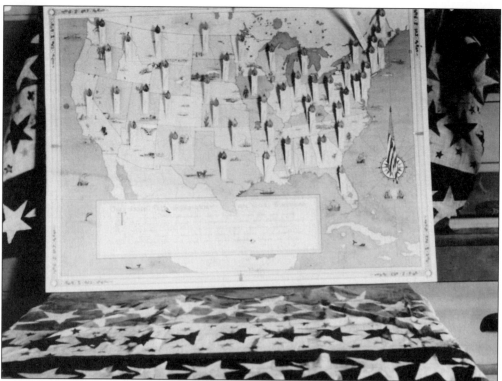
During President Coolidge's stay in South Dakota during the summer of 1927, a group of Plymouth people decided to send him this birthday card, which was about 6 square feet in size.

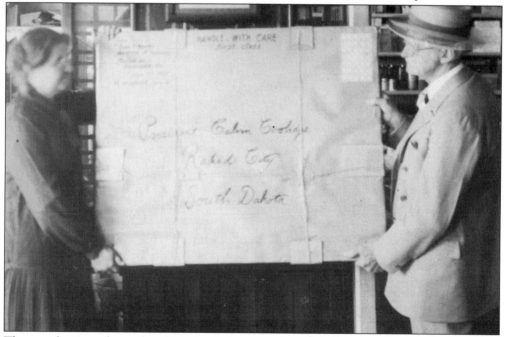
The president's card was placed inside of a huge envelope, which is shown here being displayed within the store by postmistress Florence Cilley and Vermont Governor John Weeks.

During the warm months of the year, idle locals would often sit on the porch at the store. Dan Rossiter (left) was a reporter for the *Boston Post* who often covered Plymouth. His opponent in this 1924 game of dominoes is Herbert Moore, an unofficial "greeter" at the village from the 1920s to the 1940s. Moore authored a booklet about Coolidge, and served the town as a state representative.

The store sold ice cream during the summer. The Peerless Ice Cream Company truck is parked in front of the store in this 1930s view.

Since the store was at the village center, it was often the focal point for local festivities, especially when the president visited during the 1920s. The lack of cars near the Coolidge homestead indicates that he may have been visiting there. Note the motorcycle to the left.

This view contrasts with the previous one in that there are numerous cars parked around the store building. It was probably taken at the height of a summer tourist season in the late 1920s.

On June 27, 1931, the town dedicated a memorial stone and plaque on the village green to honor its World War I veterans. The speaker's platform can be seen beneath the elm, and the honor guard in front of the Top of the Notch building. Calvin Coolidge did not attend the ceremony, as he was at his Northampton, Massachusetts, home.

This view of the store and the veterans monument was probably taken in the 1930s. The grass grows high on the green in front of a quiet store.

Many famous people passed through Plymouth during the 1920s and 1930s, either to visit the president, or to see his homestead. Noted comedian Will Rogers posed on the front steps of the store with postmistress Florence Cilley. She had postcards made of this scene, which she sold to tourists.

Will Rogers also posed at the Coolidge homestead with longtime housekeeper Aurora Pierce. It appears that Miss Pierce took the time to change into a fancy dress for the occasion.

John Wilder, Calvin Coolidge's uncle by marriage, also posed with Will Rogers while both stood in the middle of a road.

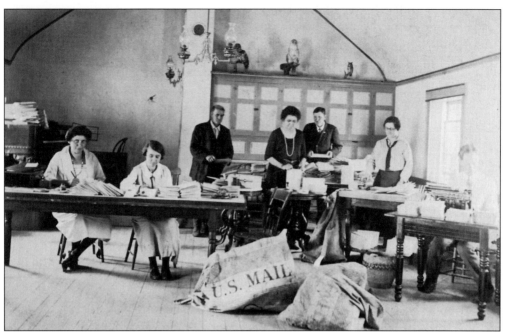

This hall, above the store, was known as Coolidge Hall, later Cilleys' Hall. It was used for many village events, including dances, reunions, suppers, and town meetings. In the view above, Florence Cilley and assistants are sorting mail for the president in the hall. During the summer of 1924, when the president stayed in Plymouth, it was used as his office, hence gaining the name "Summer White House."

This program was for a special dance held at the hall in honor of the president's inauguration in Washington, D.C., that day.

Inaugural Ball

At F. V. Cilley's Hall

(Birthplace of Our President)

PLYMOUTH, VERMONT

WEDNESDAY

March 4, 1925

Tickets, 50c per person

ADMIT ONE

By the 1930s, the hall housed a small museum of local memorabilia, including a phonograph (top center) owned by Plymouth native John G. Sargent (Coolidge's third attorney general).

The annual Pinney Hollow reunions often utilized this hall for their dinners. This view, taken c. 1900, shows the tables set for the dinner under the decorated walls.

The Nation's Most Beautiful Playhouse
LOEW'S PALACE NEWSETTE
A Local Institution With A National Reputation

Vol. 1   WASHINGTON, D. C., WEEK OF OCTOBER 31st, 1926   No. 8

Plymouth, Vermont, Old-Time Dance Orchestra, Is Stage Feature; W. C. Fields in "So's Your Old Man" on the Screen

[NEXT WEEK]

A novel and fascinating deluxe presentation program is announced for showing at LOEW'S PALACE for the week starting next Sunday afternoon, November 7, when W. C. Fields, former comedian of the Ziegfeld "Follies" and now a headliner on the silver sheet, will offer his latest Paramount screen laugh-maker, "So's Your Old Man!" as the principal photoplay attraction, while the outstanding stage offering of the bill will be the Plymouth, Vt., Old-Time Dance Orchestra, with "Uncle" John Wilder, President Coolidge's uncle, and a group of the President's boyhood friends in old-time songs and dances.

"So's Your Old Man," W. C. Fields' Paramount comedy hit, is a picturization by Gregory La Cava of Julian Street's hilarious story, "Mr. Bisbee's Princess," which won the O. Henry Memorial Prize in 1925, and in which Fields has the role of Samuel Bisbee, a hen-pecked husband who invents an unbreakable glass windshield and innocently becomes involved in an affair with a beautiful princess. The new styles that Fields inaugurates by taking off his coat at a fashionable luncheon, by his manner of playing golf and and by a dozen other ridiculous things makes "So's Your Old Man" a side-splitting delight.

From Plymouth, Vt., the home

The Plymouth Old-Time Dance Orchestra was made up of Plymouth residents, and performed at local Saturday night dances in the hall above the store for over a decade. The featured player was the president's uncle, John Wilder, who had won a fiddling contest in Boston. They toured the northeast in 1926, under the management of William Morris. Among the dance tunes they played were Lady Washington's Reel, Hull's Victory, Portland Fancy, and the Quadrille.

The orchestra members are posed in the upstairs hall at the store. Players, from left to right, are as follows: (front row) Azro Johnson, Laura Johnson, Emma Carpenter, Violet Hickory Pelkey, Eva Goodrich, Walter Lynds, Zeb Goodrich, unknown; (back row) Cassie Cady, Lynn Cady, Lewis Carpenter, John Wilder, Clarence Blanchard, and Herbert Moore.

This view of the orchestra was taken outside of the store. From left to right are Lynn Cady, John Wilder, Cassie Cady (in front of the Mason & Hamlin organ), Herbert Moore, Lewis Carpenter, and Clarence Blanchard.

This is a close-up view of the back part of the store building, as it appeared around 1940. The Elm Tree Lunch Room was operated by Herman and Violet Pelkey in the former apartment where the president was born in 1872. The porch was later removed, and the building restored to its original appearance.

This small building was located just to the left of the store-post office. During the summer months, Violet Pelkey and her husband ran an ice cream stand here. The girl in this photo is setting up the sign advertising United Farmers Peerless Ice Cream.

The orchestra did not provide the only entertainment in town. Sometimes traveling shows stopped at Plymouth. Coyne's Magic & Minstrel Show—"Two Shows in One"—stopped by in the late 1920s. The men have unpacked the tent from the 1925 Mack truck, and are completing its set-up in Aldrich's field.

Even the circus came to Plymouth! In this 1920s view, a camel and an elephant from a circus are standing in front of the store.

A circus merry-go-round horse is sitting in an open car in front of the Wilder barn.

The circus elephant is in back of a truck that bears a large ad for Socony Oil.

In the late 1800s, only this church at the Notch, and one in Tyson were left in town. This building was erected in 1840, using local lumber and iron. It was dedicated as a Congregational church in 1842. Calvin Coolidge recalled that ministers were not often retained for long periods. It is now owned by the Coolidge Memorial Foundation, which maintains its headquarters in the basement.

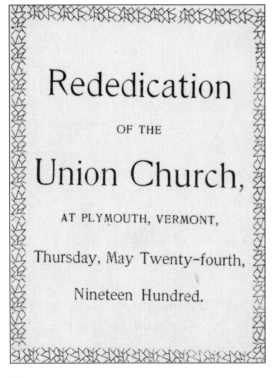

Carrie Brown Coolidge, Calvin's stepmother, was a leader of a campaign to restore this church in the late 1890s. Funds were raised by holding suppers and bake sales. The church was repaired and rededicated in 1900.

This carpenter gothic interior was built in 1900. One pew has always been marked for the use of the Coolidge family.

While Calvin Coolidge did not formally affiliate with a denomination until he went to Washington, D.C., he often attended services at this church. He and his wife are seen at the center of a crowd outside of the church, probably during the summer of 1924.

The president's father was one of the founders of this factory in the Notch in 1890. This was an outlet for the excess milk production of local dairy farmers. Charles Chapman of Ludlow erected this building, which is just past the Coolidge homestead. The president's son, John, purchased this closed business, enlarged the building, and re-opened it in 1960.

In this 1920s view, a Plymouth cheesemaker is filing some cheese off of the top as a chunk is being packaged for sale. The current cheese factory is set up so that tourists can watch part of the cheese-making process.

This stone school building served Plymouth Notch for many years until it was torn down in 1886. As Calvin Coolidge later recalled, the classroom had unpainted benches and desks. The school year consisted of three, ten-week terms, taught between May and February. This schedule left the children free to help with spring chores. In 1880, the town had sixteen schools and twenty-two teachers, with a school budget of $1,613.55.

This larger wooden building, located just above the cheese factory replaced the stone school. Some of the stones from the old school were used in the foundation of this one. This later building was closed in 1956; Plymouth built a new town-wide school at the Union village in the 1960s.

Maple sugar-making has been a popular Vermont pastime for decades; no less so in Plymouth. Healthy maple trees are tapped in March, and the sap is allowed to run into buckets. The containers were carried off, or emptied into a large basin in a wagon. Here, the president's father, John C. Coolidge, is shown pouring sap into a basin.

Lynn Cady is carrying buckets of sap into his sugarhouse. The sap was boiled down into maple syrup.

The above view shows the equipment that Plymouth sugarmaker Walter Lynds used to turn the sap into maple sugar. It takes about forty gallons of sap to produce a gallon of maple syrup. The syrup then has to be cooked to turn it into maple sugar. With added ingredients, the sugar can be formed into candy.

Several girls, led by Violet Hickory Pelkey (far right) have squirted maple syrup onto a bin of snow at Florence Cilley's farm to make "sugar on snow." The hot maple syrup would freeze into a candy-like substance. This was an early form of what would later be known as a snowcone.

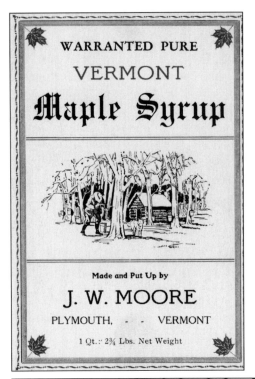
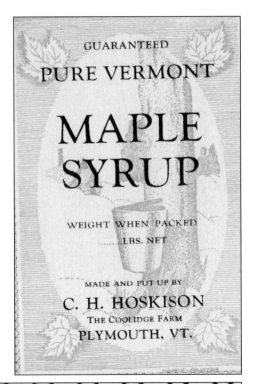
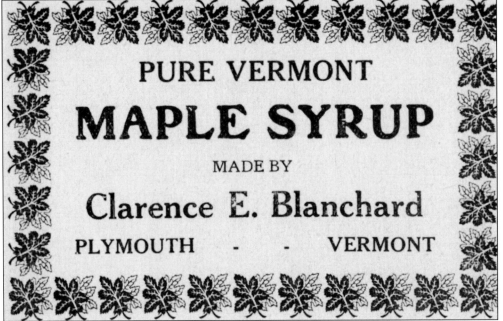

These are several labels of Plymouth maple syrup makers.

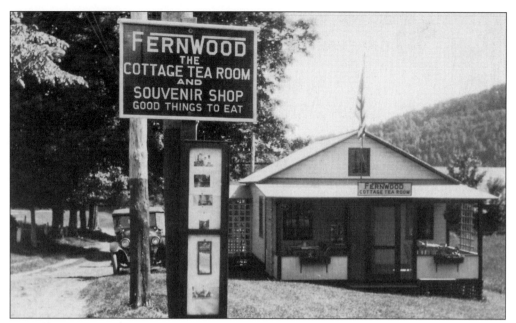

A small tea room and gift shop was located just north of the Wilder barn during the mid-1920s. The building that housed the Fernwood Tea Room is long gone, and the sign is now kept in the Aldrich house.

John C. Coolidge is standing outside of the tea room.

These views show the methods used to clear the roads of snow. They were taken at the time of John C. Coolidge's funeral in March 1926. This work was done to enable the president and his family to attend the burial service. These men are shoveling a pathway through the snow.

A small mechanical snow plow was also used to clear snow. It has a clear dome to cover the driver.

A tractor appears to be pulling the incapacitated plow.

The workmen are getting a hot refreshment in front of the Wilder barn. The snowplow is parked behind them. In spite of this work, the Coolidges had to use sleighs to get to Plymouth for the funeral.

The fourteen-room James Brown house was built at the southern edge of the village in 1869, replacing an older house. Another large barn stood behind the cameraman. Brown had thirty cows at one time. Brown was a guest at the wedding of Calvin Coolidge's parents in 1868. This home is now owned by the State of Vermont.

The only stone house in Plymouth Notch was located over the hill past the Notch schoolhouse. Owners included Azro Johnson, Charles Blanchard, and Alfred Moore; currently it is owned by the state. Wilfred Johnson and Charles Blanchard are seen with horses and dog in this c. 1901 view.

The J.W. Ayer farm was located northwest of the Stone house. This c. 1906 view shows the main house and barn; there were other barns on the property. Dell Ward (Ayer's nephew, and a childhood pal of Calvin Coolidge) is standing on the wagon. The others are Hyde Leslie, and James W. Ayer and his wife, Ella. Ayer raised Holstein cattle and hogs, and had a large orchard.

The Orin F. Ward farm, built after the Civil War, was up the road from Ayer's. A dance hall was once housed on the second floor. This building was taken down and relocated near Rutland, Vermont, before World War II.

This c. 1925 view shows four horses pulling a potato harvesting machine on a farm in Plymouth. While this was not a major local crop, the soil was more suitable for potatoes than some other vegetables.

Three
Calvin Coolidge in Plymouth

Calvin Galusha Coolidge, grandfather of the president, owned this farm on the north side of the village. He was known for raising fine horses. President Coolidge spent much time here as a boy, under the "benign influence" of his grandmother Sarah Brewer Coolidge. He recalled in his autobiography that "she had much to do with shaping the thought of my early years."

Even the attic of the old Coolidge home attracted interest. While this view might have seemed quaint to urban residents in the 1920s, it contains many objects and implements found in rural American attics. Buckets, a pegged beam, spinning wheels, a wooden grain "fan," and chairs are among the items visible.

This is the large barn on the Galusha Coolidge farm, which appears in the background of many photos of President Coolidge doing farm work. The farm is still owned by the Coolidge family.

John C. Coolidge, born in 1845, was the son of Calvin Galusha and Sarah Almeda (Brewer) Coolidge. He ran the Notch store for several years, was a justice of the peace, and sold insurance. Coolidge served his town in many positions, including both branches of the state legislature. In his autobiography, Calvin Coolidge recalled his father's talents: "If there was any physical requirement of country life which he could not perform, I do not know what it was."

A receipt from John C. Coolidge as the town tax collector in 1873.

The president's mother, born in 1846, was christened with the name of two empresses, Victoria Josephine Moor. She married John C. Coolidge in 1868. Calvin was born in 1872, and a daughter, Abbie, was born three years later. As her son recalled in his autobiography, she had a fair complexion, but that "she was practically an invalid ever after I could remember her. There was a touch of mysticism and poetry in her nature. . ." Her early death in 1885, was the first of several that would haunt the future president.

Carrie Brown was a teacher who lived in the house across from the store (later the Top of the Notch). John C. Coolidge married her in 1891. The president recalled in his autobiography that she was a devoted mother to him as "if I had been her own son." She was the village postmistress for several years around 1910, and lived to see Calvin rise as high as governor before she died in 1920.

Calvin Coolidge was the only president born on the most American holiday, the Fourth of July, in 1872. He was born upstairs in the apartment behind the store. A porch was attached to this part of the building from the 1920s to the 1950s. It now has been restored to its original rough exterior appearance.

This 1930s view shows the room in which the president was born, and its furniture. Today the furniture is located on the bottom floor of the structure, which is open to the public.

In 1876, John C. Coolidge purchased this home and the adjoining two acres from S. Butler. He paid $375.00 for it. A bay window was added, and black walnut furniture was imported from Boston for the parlor and sitting room. The water supply was spring-fed, and a privy served for sanitation. Calvin Coolidge grew up here, and often returned to visit during summers after he started his career.

The roof of the Coolidge homestead is being reshingled during the 1920s.

A group of Girl Scouts are visiting the Coolidge homestead during the 1920s. On rare occasions, President Coolidge would pose with visitors if he was at the homestead. More often, John C. Coolidge would pose.

The homestead and cheese factory appear in a typically Vermont winter scene.

This c. 1930 view shows a herd of cows passing by the Coolidge homestead on their way up the road past the school. The image serves to underline the rural nature of the president's home village.

This wooden platform appears to be a type of sawhorse. It was jokingly referred to as "Mr. Coolidge's First Platform" in a number of photographs and postcards. Calvin Coolidge stood upon it on the day before he became president, in order to work on a tree (see p. 92).

In 1932, Calvin Coolidge had a two-story addition built on the west side of the homestead. This allowed room for his books, and modern plumbing, although the only heat was supplied by fireplaces. Coolidge used this addition for only one summer before he died. This view was taken from the cheese factory.

This view of the addition to the homestead was taken from in front of the church. In the late 1950s, the addition was removed to a location near the Calvin Galusha Coolidge farm; it is still owned by the Coolidge family.

Three members of the Coolidge family can be seen in this view taken at a picnic in 1884, John C. Coolidge is sixth from the left in the back row, holding a hat against his chest. Calvin Coolidge is the boy wearing a black hat, just below a boy standing in front of his father. Calvin's sister Abigail is just above the post at the center. Carrie Brown, the future second wife of John C. Coolidge, is standing second from the right. Blanche Brown Bryant, who later wrote a booklet about Coolidge, is third from the left in the front row.

This fanciful drawing, *A Plymouth Vermont Boy About 1885*, was the work of Edward F. Paine. It was reproduced on a postcard in the 1920s. Young Calvin Coolidge is depicted hauling buckets of sap on a hilltop overlooking Plymouth. The U.S. capitol is depicted in the clouds above the village. Actually, Coolidge expected to succeed his father as the storekeeper, not become a politician!

This portrait shows Calvin Coolidge as he looked in his mid-teens.

Calvin and his sister (who died at the age of fifteen in 1890) attended the Black River Academy in Ludlow, Vermont. They followed their parents' footsteps by attending this semi-private high school. The academy building shown here was opened in 1889, the year before Coolidge graduated. It is now a museum.

After taking a term at St. Johnsbury Academy (in Vermont), Coolidge attended Amherst College (in Amherst, Massachusetts). Schoolmates included financier Dwight Morrow, and Harlan Fiske Stone, whom Coolidge would appoint as attorney general and to the Supreme Court. Coolidge graduated in the class of 1895, and went to nearby Northampton to study law with a local firm.

Coolidge began practicing law in Northampton in 1897. He soon dabbled in local politics on the ward level. He first noticed Grace Goodhue when he heard her laugh upon seeing him through a window shaving with his hat on. He arranged to meet her, and told her he did that to keep an unruly lock of hair in place. She was a native of Burlington, Vermont, and a graduate of the University of Vermont. Grace taught at the Clarke School for the Deaf. She possessed a charming personality, causing many to wonder what she saw in her reticent suitor. They were married at her parent's home on October 4, 1905. In his autobiography, Coolidge stated that "for almost a quarter of a century she has borne with my infirmities, and I have rejoiced in her graces." Since her husband was often away on legal business or political activity, Grace Coolidge had to assume the major burden of raising her two sons. She is shown adjusting the weathervane in the garden across from the Coolidge homestead in Plymouth.

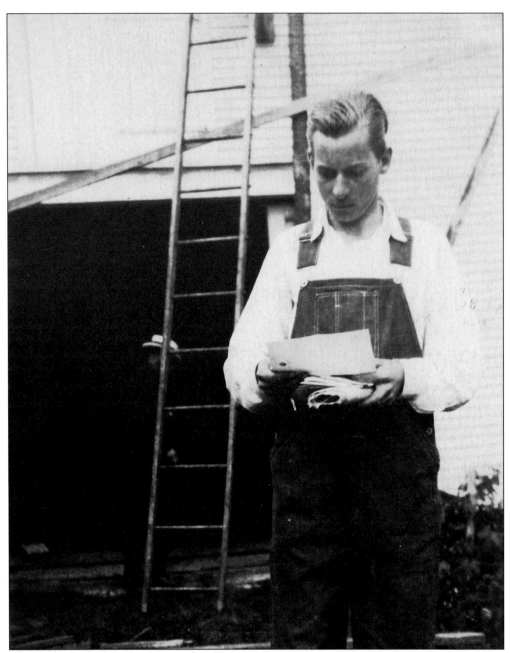

A few months after they were married, the Coolidges settled into a duplex in Northampton, where they resided until 1930. On September 7, 1906, their first son, John, was born. He was to be educated in Northampton schools, Mercersberg Academy (in Pennsylvania), and Amherst College. In 1929, he married Florence Trumbull, the daughter of a Connecticut governor, and they raised two daughters in her home state. John Coolidge had a career as a business executive. He has written forewords to books about his father. At the age of ninety, John Coolidge still summered in Plymouth, and was active in the Calvin Coolidge Memorial Foundation. He is seen here reading his mail while standing in front of the Coolidge homestead when the roof was being reshingled in the 1920s.

The Coolidges' second son was born on April 13, 1908. A bright student, he inherited his mother's outgoing personality, and his father's (repressed) sense of mischief. Like his brother, he attended Northampton schools, and Mercersberg Academy. When his father became president, he was working as a tobacco picker on a farm near Northampton. When a fellow worker told him that if his father became president, he wouldn't be working in a tobacco field, Calvin Jr. reportedly replied, "If my father were your father, you would." This portrait of Calvin Coolidge Jr. was taken when he was sixteen, just before his death.

This view of three generations of Coolidges was taken in front of the homestead, around 1922.

This group photo shows Calvin Coolidge dressed in his farm smock. He is holding an old family heirloom musket.

Calvin Coolidge had a steady rise in Massachusetts politics. After serving as a city councilor and clerk of courts, he was elected to the state House of Representatives for two terms. In 1910/11, he was mayor of Northampton, then was elected to four terms in the State Senate. After serving as the presiding officer of that body in his last two terms, he was elected lieutenant governor for three terms (1916–1919). Coolidge then was elected governor for two terms (1919–1921). The highlight of his governorship was his role in quelling the violence after the Boston police strike of 1919. Coolidge's statement that "there is no right to strike against the public safety by any body, any time, any where" made him a hero on the national scene. This portrait of Coolidge as governor was sent to people who requested a picture of him.

Friends of Coolidge mounted a campaign to net him the Republican nomination for president in 1920. He discouraged this, and received scant support at the convention. Senator Warren G. Harding was nominated as a compromise candidate. The convention delegates rejected the Senatorial cabal's nominee for the second spot on the ticket, choosing Coolidge after an Oregon judge nominated him. This postcard was one of a pair showing the two Republican nominees in 1920.

Calvin and Grace Coolidge are in the foreground at this reception held for him at Plymouth in July, 1920. John C. Coolidge sent out postcards of this scene to those who had sent him cards congratulating him on his son's nomination.

Coolidge conducted a speaking tour of the upper South during the campaign. Harding and Coolidge swamped the Democratic ticket of James Cox and Franklin D. Roosevelt. Harding set a precedent by inviting Coolidge to sit in on his cabinet meetings. Coolidge's main duties as vice-president were to preside over the Senate, and make speeches for the administration.

During the summer of 1923, President Harding went on his ill-fated speaking tour in the western states. Calvin Coolidge went to Plymouth with his wife for a vacation. President Harding fell ill on his way back from Alaska. Vice-President Coolidge is seen doctoring a tree at the homestead on August 2, 1923, not suspecting that Warren G. Harding would die suddenly a few hours later.

News of Harding's death was brought to Plymouth in the early morning hours of August 3 by messenger. The new president decided to have his father, a notary public, administer the oath of office to him. Only a few people (no photographers) were present to witness this event at 2:47 AM. In this depiction of the event by artist Guido Boer, the three Coolidges are in the center.

The Lincoln Drape-style lamp shown here illuminated the "Homestead Inaugural," but oddly, Coolidge did not make use of the family bible.

John C. Coolidge is seen in the room where the swearing-in took place. This room, along with much of the homestead, can now be seen via a self-guided tour.

Characteristically, Calvin Coolidge went back to bed after his swearing-in, and he slept for a few hours! That morning, he and Grace got into a car, and were driven to the village cemetery, where he made a "devotional visit" to his mother's grave. They proceeded to Rutland, Vermont, where they boarded a train to go to Washington, D.C., as shown here.

Coolidge let it be known that he would seek a full term as president in the 1924 election. He deftly avoided any tarnish from the Teapot Dome scandals leftover from his predecessor's administration. Coolidge's opposition in the early primary elections was swept aside, so that he was considered a shoe-in at the Republican Party convention. Slogans such as "Keep Cool with Coolidge" were already current, as can be seen from this campaign postcard.

The 1924 Republican Convention, held in Cleveland, Ohio, was the first to be broadcast over radio. A radio set was brought in for John C. Coolidge to use to hear the broadcast of his son's nomination.

Calvin Coolidge Jr. raised a blister on his toe when playing tennis with his brother at the White House. He developed blood poisoning, and died on July 7. His father later wrote that, "when he went, the power and the glory of the Presidency went with him." This view shows a Boy Scout honor guard at the grave of Calvin Coolidge Jr.

Coolidge did not wish to wage an aggressive election campaign, in spite of having both Democratic (John W. Davis) and Progressive (Robert LaFollette) opponents. He spent much of that summer at Plymouth. This provided photographers with many chances to snap views of Coolidge "in action," such as this one of him and Grace stepping out of a limousine.

Coolidge is seen here riding his horse, Captain. Anything the president did was a "photo opportunity."

This view was taken in the upstairs hall at the Cilley Store, which was used as Coolidge's "office" while he stayed in Plymouth. Coolidge is seated at the center, with his presidential secretary, C. Bascom Slemp, standing on the left. Seated on the right is the presidential stenographer, Erwin Geisser.

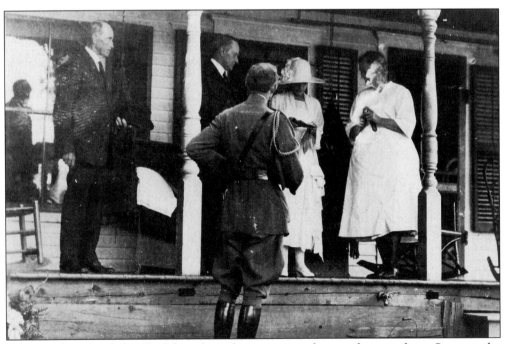

Anyone who visited the Coolidges drew the attention of news photographers. Seen on the piazza of the homestead, this group includes (from the left) John C. Coolidge, Calvin Coolidge, a military aide, Grace Coolidge, and an unidentified woman.

Grace Coolidge came in for her share of attention from newsmen while at Plymouth. She tried to maintain gardens at the Coolidge Homestead that were begun by Calvin's mother, and kept up by his stepmother. In this view, she is next to some flowers, with the homestead barn in the background.

Here, Grace Coolidge is walking toward the homestead with a bodyguard; the Wilder barn is in the background.

John C. Coolidge was also drew the attention of photographers. In this c. 1922 scene, he is standing with Calvin Jr., who is dressed in a long sweater and a boy's cap of the era.

John Coolidge, dressed in overalls, is driving a wagon past the homestead with his grandfather. Another time, Earle Bryant once drove his car over an embankment to avoid hitting these two John Coolidges in their horse-drawn buggy!

Both Calvin Coolidge (in his autobiography) and his son John noted that John C. Coolidge enjoyed the attention he received after Calvin became president. Gifts like the loaf of bread being presented to him here may have added to John C. Coolidge's enjoyment of visitors. The truck is from the Goddard Monadnock Bread Co., of Claremont, New Hampshire.

John C. Coolidge's abilities as a handyman were of great interest to the mostly urban news photographers. He is shown here filing a wood shingle, which was a common form of exterior siding on barns and some houses in that region.

President Coolidge's elderly aunt and uncle lived in the Wilder house. Their rustic appearance attracted the interest of photographers. She was Gratia Moor Wilder, sister of the president's mother. She is talking with her famous nephew, who is dressed in his farmer's smock.

Coolidge's Uncle John Wilder was a farmer. He is sitting on the town cannon, used to fire salutes on the Fourth of July. A bone of contention between the Notch and Union villages, it was often kept in John Wilder's barn. Calvin Coolidge reportedly was involved in one "theft" of the cannon as a young man.

Calvin Coolidge had been shy as a boy, and never completely overcame this as an adult. He carried on the pressing of flesh expected of politicians, but often without enthusiasm. During the summer of 1924, many people traveled to Plymouth to see the president; a few were lucky enough to meet him. Delegations such as this one were often allowed a quick pose for a photo. Calvin and Grace Coolidge are sixth and seventh from the right in this view, taken at the homestead.

Vermonters were not loathe to share in the attention accorded their president. Coolidge is shaking hands with former Vermont Governor Percival Clement. Grace Coolidge may be holding the flowers to avoid the chore of handshaking.

Coolidge is shown with local resident Henry Brown (left), and Earle Kinsley (right). Kinsley, from Rutland, was a Republican National Committeeman for Vermont during the Coolidge years.

President Coolidge probably didn't mind some of the "photo opportunities" with local residents. Dan McCuin, the "Plymouth Midget," is shaking hands with the president. Some newspapers captioned this view "the biggest man in the country shaking hands with the smallest."

Grace Coolidge is shaking hands with Civil War veteran Frank Joslin (or Josselyn), of Tyson. Joslin was reported to have voted Republican for the first time in his life to support Harding and Coolidge in 1920.

Inventor Thomas Edison, tire-maker Harvey Firestone, and auto-magnate Henry Ford often traveled together during summer vacations. In August 1924, they visited the president while on a New England trip. Coolidge is watching while Edison is examining one of the cameras to be used to photograph the group.

Henry Ford is examining two old rakes shown to him by the Coolidges. Ford was very interested in old-style implements; he founded the Greenfield Village Museum in Michigan to preserve rural American artifacts.

Photographer George Chalmers' young son is apparently being handed a coin by Henry Ford. Coolidge is behind Ford, and Harvey Firestone is at the far right. Several newspapermen are standing in the background.

Young Chalmers is holding a camera. In back of him. from the left, are Harvey Firestone, Ford, Edison, Russell Firestone, and Grace and John C. Coolidge.

Knowing that Henry Ford collected old things for his restored village, Calvin Coolidge decided to give him a wooden sap bucket. He is showing it to the newspapermen.

The two Coolidges are standing next to the bucket, in front of the homestead piazza. Henry Ford and Thomas Edison are to the right of the bucket.

It appears that the whole group wanted to pose on the piazza when Coolidge was going to autograph the bucket and present it to Ford. However, some of the participants' faces would have been obscured from view by the pillars. To help the photographers, the chairs were set up on the lawn in front of the barn.

Members of the group are, from the left: Harvey Firestone, Calvin Coolidge, Henry Ford, Thomas Edison, Russell Firestone (standing), Grace Coolidge, and John C. Coolidge. When Calvin Coolidge handed the bucket to Ford, he reportedly said, "My father had it, I used it, and now you've got it!" Edison and John C. Coolidge also signed the bucket.

109

Photographers never tired of snapping Calvin Coolidge carrying out farm chores. Coolidge did know how to do these things, and no doubt he realized the value of being seen performing them. It reinforced his image as a down-home American. Coolidge, wearing his farming smock, is pulling on his boots.

John, Calvin, and John C. Coolidge are standing next to a haying machine at the old Calvin Galusha Coolidge farm. Scenes like this, with the president in his farming smock, were meant to encourage farmers to support him. Many of them had fallen on hard times in the early 1920s.

Calvin Coolidge is operating the horse-drawn hay rake. The large barn in the background is at the Calvin Galusha Coolidge farm.

Coolidge is pitching hay into a horse-drawn wagon, with the help of a hired hand. The hay would be stored in a barn to be used as feed for the horses and cows.

Calvin Coolidge is carrying out the important farm chore of sharpening the blade of a scythe, used to cut grass.

Here, Calvin Coolidge is cutting grass with a small sickle.

Another classic farm chore was milking a cow. Here, neither Coolidge nor the cow look very enthusiastic about it!

Here, Calvin Coolidge is plowing the field in front of the Calvin Galusha Coolidge home. This is being done the old fashioned way; with horses pulling the long-handled plow, while Coolidge steers it.

Calvin Coolidge is chopping wood with an axe. The split wood was used for fuel for the woodstove or fireplace in the homestead.

Coolidge is using a grinding wheel to sharpen a scythe blade.

Sometimes, news photographers convinced Coolidge pose on the farm when he was not prepared to. Here, he is standing next to the hay wagon, with a pitchfork in his hand, but still dressed in his "street" clothes.

Coolidge is piloting the hay rake in his street clothes; something seems to have gotten into his eye. When pictures like these were published, pundits would criticize Coolidge's appearing to be a phony farmer in "city clothes."

Charles G. Dawes was a Chicago banker, who had been active in Republican politics since 1896. He had served as Harding's first director of the Bureau of the Budget, and headed the commission which established the Dawes Plan for German reparations after World War I. The colorful Dawes was nominated as Coolidge's running mate on the 1924 Republican ticket. Due to the death of Coolidge's son, and the president's natural reticence, Dawes carried most of the burden of speechmaking for the ticket. Dawes delivered a mild rebuke to the Ku Klux Klan in a speech at Augusta, Maine, on August 23, 1924. Then he visited Coolidge in Plymouth, where they posed in the doorway of the homestead barn. Coolidge is wearing a black armband in mourning for his deceased son.

During the 1924 election campaign, the Republican Party sent trucks in a tour through much of the country. These were decorated with bunting, and posters of the party's national ticket, Coolidge and Dawes. John C. Coolidge is looking at one of the trucks in front of the store.

Not to be out-done, a car bedecked with Progressive Party banners also visited Plymouth. This third party nominated Wisconsin Senator Robert LaFollette, who made a respectable showing in spite of an under-funded campaign.

In the spring of 1924, a number of Coolidge's friends and neighbors formed the Home Town Coolidge Club of Plymouth Vermont. The officers, all Plymouth residents, were as follows: Edward J. Blanchard as president, Clarence L. Keith as vice president, George W. Frink as second vice-president, Dick P. Brown as secretary, and Mrs. Laura Johnson as treasurer. A $1 donation bought a colorful pin, a membership card and certificate, and a booklet about Coolidge. The pin is shown here (enlarged).

This is the charter membership card for the Home Town Coolidge Club. In spite of the third party candidacy of Robert LaFollette, Coolidge and Dawes won the election handily, with 15,718,789 votes to 8,378,962 for Davis and Bryan, and 4,822,319 for LaFollette and Wheeler.

The Hometown Coolidge Club also produced a song, "Keep Cool and Keep Coolidge," which became well-known around the country. This is the front page of one version of the sheet music.

In 1925, President Coolidge elevated his attorney general, Harlan Fiske Stone, to the Supreme Court. The Senate would not confirm Coolidge's first nominee to replace Stone, so he nominated his fellow Plymouth native John Garibaldi Sargent to the post. Sargent, a huge man, had carried on a law practice in Ludlow, and served a term as Attorney General of Vermont. He won unanimous acceptance for the federal post.

During his second term, Coolidge was able to spend little time in Plymouth. He visited there briefly in August 1925, when this view was taken of him, his wife, and father leaving the Plymouth church one Sunday. John C. Coolidge fell ill not long after this visit.

May (or Mae) Johnson was John C. Coolidge's nurse during his final illness in the winter of 1925–26. Dr. A. M. Cram (of Bridgewater) was Coolidge's family physician. They are shown on the front piazza of the Coolidge homestead. John C. Coolidge turned down his son's offer to stay at the White House. He died suddenly on March 18, 1926.

After the end of his full term as president in 1929, Coolidge retired to private life. He did serve on a few committees, traveled some, and wrote articles, a newspaper column, and an autobiography. Coolidge spent part of each summer in Plymouth. Here, Grace Coolidge is examining his old baby pram in front of the homestead.

121

Coolidge tried to avoid contact with tourists as much as possible. On quiet days, he would sit on the homestead piazza and watch people go by.

Sometimes, Grace would join Calvin on the piazza, and work on her knitting.

While in the White House, the Coolidges acquired a couple of pet dogs: Tiny Tim (a red chow) and Prudence Prim (a white collie). The chow is in this view, taken in 1931. The Coolidges are standing next the World War monument dedicated earlier that year.

Here, the Coolidges are in front of the homestead with the collie. This dog became famous by being posed in a well-known painting of Grace Coolidge wearing her red dress.

Calvin Coolidge died of a heart attack at his Northampton, Massachusetts home on January 5, 1933, at the age of sixty. He had told a friend a few weeks before his death, "I no longer fit in with these times." After a funeral service in Northampton, he was buried in the family plot in the Notch cemetery. A soldier is guarding the grave, which has flowers placed around it.

This is a close-up of the graves of Calvin Coolidge and Calvin Coolidge Jr. Other than the presidential seal, there is nothing on the stone to distinguish Calvin Coolidge's grave from many others. Grace Coolidge survived him by twenty-four years.

Efforts in Plymouth to commemorate Coolidge began shortly after his death. This view shows the memorial service held at the Notch cemetery on August 3, 1934, the eleventh anniversary of his accession to the presidency. Such events were held intermittently over the years, until the Calvin Coolidge Memorial Foundation was chartered in 1960. This Plymouth-based group sponsors a ceremony at Coolidge's grave every year on July Fourth (Coolidge's birthday), and holds its annual meeting in the village church on the first Sunday in August, with a guest speaker about Coolidge and his ideals.

This is the front cover of the program for the memorial service held at Plymouth Notch on August 3, 1934.

This small memorial service for Calvin Coolidge was held on July 4, 1944. Several military veterans and local residents are seen at the laying of a wreath on the president's grave.

Sources

Aldrich, Lewis Cass and Holmes, Frank B., eds. *History of Windsor County, Vermont.* Syracuse, NY: D. Mason & Co., 1891.

Booraem, Hendrik V. *The Provincial: Calvin Coolidge and His World, 1885–1895.* Cranbury, NJ: Bucknell University Press, Associated University Presses, 1994.

Bryant, Blanche Brown. *Calvin Coolidge As I Knew Him.* DeLeon Springs, FL: E.O. Painter Printing Co., 1971.

Child, Hamilton, comp. *Gazetteer and Business Directory of Windsor County, Vermont, for 1883–84.* Syracuse, NY: Journal Office, 1884.

Coolidge, Calvin. *The Autobiography of Calvin Coolidge.* New York: Cosmopolitan Book, Corp., 1929.

Coolidge, John. Interview by author, September 1996.

Fuess, Claude. *Calvin Coolidge: The Man From Vermont.* Boston, MA: Little Brown & Co., 1940.

Lathem, Edward Connery, ed. *Your Son, Calvin Coolidge.* Montpelier, VT: Vermont Historical Society, 1968.

Ward, Eliza; Mahon, Barbara; and Chiolino, Barbara. *A Plymouth Album.* Randolph, VT: Greenhills Books, 1983.